Stephen Hawking

A Stephen Hawking Biography

The Greatest Scientist of Our Time

Michael Woodford

Table of Contents

A brief history of Stephen Hawking

Dennis William Sciama (1926 – 1999) was a don at the University of Cambridge in the United Kingdom. He was one of the most eminent physicists of his time.

In 1963 he was informed that he was to receive a new pupil, a young man from Oxford who wished to undertake his doctoral thesis under his tutelage.

There was nothing unusual in this. Mentoring new pupils was part and parcel of a university academic's life.

However the new pupil seemed, on the face of it, unremarkable. In fact he had the reputation of a lazy and somewhat difficult student.

In his written exam at Oxford he had achieved neither a first nor a second degree. A first would have entitled him to undertake postgraduate studies at Cambridge; a second at Oxford.

He had to submit to an oral exam, an ordeal that terrified him but nevertheless impressed his examiners who remarked that they faced intelligence greater than there on.

After a while Sciama also agreed that he was dealing with a highly potent intellect.

This man was only 21 years old and moreover had just been given 2 years to live.

His name was Stephen William Hawking.

Hawking was born on January 8 1942 in Oxford, to Frank and Isobel (nee Walker) Hawking. He has two younger sisters, Phillipa and Mary, and an adopted brother, Edward.

Both parents were academics at Oxford University when Stephen was born. Frank read medicine while Isobel read philosophy politics and economics.

Frank would become head of the parasitology department at the National Medical Institute, London, in 1950.

But at the time of Stephen's birth the family was not prosperous. Frank's grandfather had bankrupted the Hawkings by incautious purchases during the Great Depression. It was only his wife that had saved them from utter disaster by opening a school in their home.

Isobel was the son of a Glasgow doctor who was determined to send her daughter to university at a time when an academic career (or a career of any kind beyond being in service, nursing or teaching) was considered highly unusual for women.

Oxford University did not even award degrees to women until 1920.

Perhaps it was this scape with ruin that made Frank Hawking a highly meticulous and methodical young man.

Isobel was more adventurous and hated being hemmed in.

When she was in confinement at hospital with Stephen (she was in her final week) she left the hospital and amused herself window shopping in the Oxford streets.

She went into a bookstore and there bought an astronomical atlas. Reflecting on the career her son would take, she regarded this as a propitious purchase.

The Hawkings were a bookish and somewhat eccentric family. Often meals would be spent in entire silence while Dad. Mom and Stephen read at table.

The family travelled in an old London cab, kept bees in the basement and made fireworks in the glasshouse. And Frank's specialty, tropical diseases, must have made for fascinating discussions over dinner, when they weren't all reading, of course.

Frank wanted Stephen to follow him into medicine, but Stephen had other ideas.

The boy loved science, and was often observed looking up on a starry night, lost in wonder.

Stephen was a very active lad. He was sociable, and loved to climb, play games and to dance.

As a student he was bright, though considered unexceptional. It may be that he considered the curriculum unchallenging, or else he did not have a strong enough focus for his mind. The latter would seem to be borne out by his university experiences.

The family moved to St Albans, a small city lying just to the north of London, when Stephen was eight.

He attended St Albans School. This all boys' institution is now fee paying, and is one of the oldest independent schools in the United Kingdom.

At the time of Stephen's education, however, it was a direct grant school. This meant that a number of students were awarded places on the basis of successful scholarship applications, whilst for others, normal fees were paid.

St Albans during the 1950s was a mixed bag of a school. It sported the astonishingly inappropriate motto 'Mediocria firma' – which translates as 'the middle way is safest'.

The motto was taken from the bi-sexual Elizabethan philosopher Francis Bacon, and caused Stephen's headmaster – WT Marsh – agonies of internal contradiction.

The man was duty bound the exhort, the traditions of the dictum whilst being horrified by association of the words with mediocrity – the last characteristic with which a school such as St Albans would wish to be associated.

(In fact, the adage related to the risky Elizabethan times, when to stray from the center ground could be seen as politically threatening, and would as like as not land the protagonist in serious, life threatening, danger.)

St Albans School in the 1950s was a somewhat eccentric place. A mixture of Masters and (occasionally) Mistresses taught the boys.

These teachers were intellectually extremely able, and may well have inspired the young Stephen onto future academic brilliance, but also bizarre in their behavior.

The cane was wielded widely, and not only by adults. Prefects were perfectly at liberty to beat boys who crossed boundaries – or not, in many cases.

In fact, an air of violence simmered beneath the surface of the old institution. WT Marsh would routinely lash out at students who annoyed him – a left wing sixth form poet often bearing the brunt of his anger.

He once used the death in a cycling accident of an old boy of the school as an opportunity for a brief lesson in the proper meaning of tragedy.

He described the young man's death as sad for his parents, but not tragic. That must have been a great comfort to them!

As a boy at St Albans, the young Stephen was given to what today we might consider creative but slightly offbeat behavior.

Whilst organized sports – as important to schools such as St Albans today as they were in the 1950s – held little appeal, he would create complex board games involving fantasy battles.

A kind of forerunner to Dungeons and Dragons.

In a harsh environment, only the strongest survive. St Albans was such a place, as were many fee charging schools of the time.

Those who opted out of the military aspect of schooling – it was possible to do so, but difficult – were routinely humiliated. They were given the task of building a Greek Ampitheatre at one point.

The task involving not only physically very challenging work (remember, they were still quite young boys) but to be carried out dressed just in shorts and t shirt – whatever the weather.

And although every single boy had passed a tough entrance examination to gain entry to the school – even those not in receipt of direct funding – to be cast in the bottom stream was considered academic failure.

Stephen was certainly not in this category. He sat comfortably half way through the A sets. If this seems surprising for a man who would become known as a genius, it is perhaps not that surprising.

St Albans and the surrounding region had seen a mass influx of European and Jewish immigrants during and after World War Two. Many of these families had trained their sons to achieve success at a school such as St Albans.

They possessed perhaps a work ethic and tolerance of the system that Stephen did not. The young Hawking also had a very eccentric mind, creative beyond the limits of the curriculum.

Whilst he certainly engaged with many of the very intellectual teachers, the curriculum of the time would offer little inspiration to him, being geared almost exclusively to winning an Oxbridge scholarship.

He was also a boy who liked to challenge the systems at St Albans. When older, he organized ban the bomb marches to Aldermaston, where the UK's chemical and biological warfare weapons are now developed.

Whilst Stephen did undertake the officer cadet training at the school, he did so with a kind of charming defiance, for example by refusing to keep his uniform smart.

And when on the firing range, long term hearing issues were far from the teachers' minds – it was seen as a weakness to require ear plugs.

However, quite happy to be regarded thus, Stephen created his own pair from blotting paper, which he stuffed so far down his ears that they had to be removed by the doctor the following day.

He as a small boy, and as such was a natural target for the bullying that prevailed at the school.

It seems as though he took it well enough, relying on his quick wit to put down the bigger boys, and accepting that sometimes he would escape, sometimes not.

In this simmering cauldron of a school, where explosions were always just around the corner, Stephen drew inspiration from his math master, Dick Tahta.

With the Armenian teacher, he built an early computer from discarded electronics.

And it is hard to argue against the ambience of the school leading Stephen on his journey to becoming the genius that lives today.

Although, it might have been his desire to be different from the norm that offered the greatest inspiration.

His parents were keen to give him an education as they had had, and he enrolled in the University of Oxford in1959, when he was only 17.

Oxford University is the oldest university in the English speaking, dating back to at least 1096 but probably much older than that.

The university was so prestigious and important in the life of the United Kingdom that until 1950 it elected two members to the British House of Commons.

The University has 38 colleges, to which in the Oxford and Cambridge Universities students must be affiliated.

Hawking joined the oldest of the Oxford colleges, University College. That college produced such men and women as the British Prime Minister Clement Atlee, US President Bill Clinton, the poet Percy Bysshe Shelley and the violinist Sophie Solomon.

Hawking enjoyed university life. He especially enjoyed the social life, as of course many university students do. He joined a rowing team as a coxswain. It was said that he was a somewhat enthusiastic, if not reckless, coxswain, losing oars and getting the team into dangerous scrapes.

And as is the case for many university students his studies tended to take second place.

He was bright and he knew it. He could write essays and take exams with a minimum effort and often with little, if any preparation.

While this got him through university he suffered from lack of application. His professors and tutors would comment on his lack of focus and carelessness.

It was only in his final year, 1963 that he realized he needed to focus on his energies and make up his mind what he wanted to do with an Oxford education.

In his final exam Hawking gained neither a First (qualification to undertake postgraduate studies at Oxford) nor a Second (to Cambridge). This necessitated an oral examination which Hawking regarded with trepidation.

Nevertheless he applied himself to the task and managed to achieve a Second. This was what he earnestly desired. He wanted to study for his doctorate under the tutelage of the great Cambridge physicist and cosmologist, Fred Hoyle.

But he was to be greeted by disappointment.

Reaching For the Stars

Sir Fred Hoyle (1915 – 2001) was a
Cambridge University don and one of the
foremost, if not the eminent astronomer of
his day.

At a time when cosmology, the study of the
origins and evolution of the universe, was in
its infancy Hoyle was propelling it forward.

The idea that the universe was millions of
years old and developed by physical laws
and not by the direct intervention of a deity
was still comparatively new.

In 1897 the famous physicist Lord Kelvin
had proposed that Earth itself was probably
around 20 million years old. We now know

that estimate is ludicrously short, not nearly long enough to account for the formation of the world and evolution of life. Today scientists believe that close to 4 billion years is a more accurate estimation.

But how old was the universe itself?

Hoyle went part way to calculate an age by his work on stellar nucleosynthesis, that is, the formation and evolution of stars.

He showed that stars were formed by the coalescence of gas clouds under gravity. These dense clouds produced a colossal nuclear reaction that formed a star.

Moreover, as these stars run out of fuel they expand into such entities as red giants, and then collapse into smaller stars with colossal gravitational pull, such as white dwarves.

This evolution demonstrated that the universe had to be many billions of years old. Our Sun, for example, formed about 4 and a half billon years ago and is expected to last enough 10 billion years.

But stellar nucleosynthesis does not in itself tell us how old the universe itself is, nor does it answer an obvious accompanying question – did the universe have an origin and if so, how did it come into being?

This is of course the question that has absorbed humanity from its very inception. For centuries it belonged to the realms of religion and philosophy.

With the advent of science as we understand it in 16th and 17th century Europe were able to begin to answer how the universe functioned but still not how it came into being – if at all.

Its existence was still attributed to some supernatural creative principle, whether it was a personal God or an impersonal one who created and sustained the universe but without taking any interest in it.

In 1917 Albert Einstein proposed that the universe was static and essentially unchanging, implying that it had no origin.

Later he changed his mind after the famous astronomer Edwin Hubble (1889 – 1953), after whom of course the space telescope is named, observed that apparent clouds of gas in space called nebulae were actually galaxies, and appeared to be receding into space.

From this he deduced that objects in the observable universe were actually expanding away from each other.

Einstein adjusted his own theory in order to account for this, but still the apparent expansion could not be satisfactorily explained.

Enter Fred Hoyle. He agreed with Einstein that the universe was indeed essentially static and unchanging.

Stars were born and died, of course. But as a body is ordered and balanced by physical laws; the universe remained static. He called this model of the universe the Steady State Theory.

How then did Hoyle explain the apparent expansion of the universe? He supposed, without any definitive proof, that matter was continually being created in the spaces between galaxies.

So the universe was something like a pool of paint expanding because paint from a can is being continuously and evenly poured into it.

The Steady State Theory neatly avoids the problem of the origin of the universe by stating it never had one. The universe is eternal.

Apart from other scientific objections which are perhaps too complex to explore now, the theory does not answer the obvious question of how can something be produced from nothing?

This of course is a question that theologians are asked as well. And it was a question that was to be – and remains – the focus of Hawking's research.

Nevertheless Steady State Theory was widely accepted during the 50s and 60s, riding largely on the prestige of Hoyle.

Understandably Hawking was anxious to anxious to secure Hoyle's tutelage for his doctorate thesis.

However it was not to be.

Besides being a giant of astronomy and physics Hoyle was something of a scientific celebrity, much as Hawking would be.

He was constantly touring and giving lectures, being interviewed, writing, and using his status to intervene in fields often outside of his level of expertise.

For example, he famously entered the lists against paleontologists by in 1986 claiming that fossils of Archaeopteryx, a creature with affinities of both birds and reptiles and thus regarded as transitional between the two, were fake.

In the 1970s Hoyle proposed that life did not originate on Earth but instead evolved from microbes in meteors and comets that have struck Earth.

He curiously suggested that sudden and violent pandemics such as the 1918 Influenza Epidemic and the 1986 Mad Cow Disease outbreak in the United Kingdom were evidence of alien attacks.

Hoyle would have made an unsuitable tutor, being difficult to pin down and prone to going on tangents and fanciful ventures, none of which undermined his undoubted scientific prowess in the field of physics.

And there may have been another reason why Hoyle did not take young Hawking under his wing.

On one occasion Hawking was listening to Fred Hoyle lecturing at the Royal Society. At one point he interrupted Hoyle to correct him on something he saying.

Hoyle was astonished to hear someone who had barely graduated confidently daring to correct him, and must have been even more astonished to discover that Hawking was right.

So young Hawking got Denis Sciama.

Sciama had definite advantages over Hoyle that Hawking really needed at that time.

Sciama was brilliant, like Hoyle, but was not a celebrity. He was dependable.

Further he was genuinely solicitous for his students. He was encouraging and supportive, and recognized Hawking's unique intellect and also saw that it needed to be developed.

Hawking was in sore need of encouragement, for he had just been diagnosed with Amyotrophic lateral sclerosis (ALS), also known as Motor neuron disease or Lou Gehrig's disease.

This affliction is characterized by the normally rapid deterioration of muscle function leading to death.

The cause of the disease is unknown and there is no cure.

Hawking was already beginning to lose control of his body. He had falls and his speech was beginning to slur.

With his doctors giving him 2 years to live and faced with a horrible and humiliating decline, Hawking was depressed and in need of a reason to carry on.

He found comfort in his wife, Jane Wilde. The two had met at a News Years party at Cambridge. They became engaged in October 1964 and married on July 14 1965.

Hawking said that the marriage gave him 'something to live for', but before this Sciama encouraged the depressed young man to focus on his thesis.

Hawking chose as the topic for his thesis a theory of the origin of the universe – an ambitious task for a graduate!

He chose to contradict the mind that he had wanted as his tutor – Fred Hoyle. He did not wish to defend Steady State Theory. Rather he chose to advocate the other great theory of the origin of the universe – the Big Bang.

The father of the Big Bang theory was a Belgian priest, physicist and mathematician, Georges Lemaitres.

In 1927 Lemaitres explained the apparent expansion of the universe by positing that all matter had originally been condensed in a single point – a singularity.

This singularity then expanded, forming the universe which is still speeding outwards from the point when the singularity 'exploded'.

This idea came to be adopted by a number of physicists and astronomers who believed it best fitted the observable facts.

The theory had the advantage of not having to explain the creation of new matter, for all the matter that ever was contained in the primeval singularity.

However it could not explain what caused the initial expansion of the singularity. If all matter was contained in the singularity then what caused it to explode?

Further it did not explain where that matter comes from in the first place.

We casually and not entirely correctly use the word 'explode' but ironically Fred Hoyle used this terminology to condemn the idea.

In a 1949 radio interview he referred to the theory of a universe expanding outward from a single point as the 'Big Bang;' theory. And of course the name has stuck, the idea fiercest opponent actually giving the theory its name.

A major problem for the Big Bang theorists was proposing a mechanism. How could the entire mass of the universe be contained in a single point? There was no model, and no observable object in the universe that could provide a clue.

Nevertheless Albert Einstein had envisaged the possibility of singularities in his 1915 General Theory of Relativity.

In broad terms the General Theory of Relativity holds that there is no fixed object in the universe. Everything is in motion and is in motion relative to the motion of everything else. So a bird flying moves in relation to the movement of the air, which in turn is relative to the movement of the earth, the movement of the sun, of the solar system, the Milky Way, and so forth.

From this fairly straight forward observation Einstein extrapolated principles for time and matter.

For example, he concluded that as there was no fixed object, there was no fixed point of time either. Time was fluid.

From his General Theory of Relativity Einstein came up with a Special Theory of Relativity, which stated that energy and mass were mutually convertible. He composed the famous equation $E=MC^2$; an object is convertible to an amount of energy equivalent to the mass of that object multiplied by the speed of light squared.

We see an awful demonstration of this principle in nuclear fission, when an atomic bomb explodes, thought General and Special Relativity have a plethora of applications in the field of physics.

The young Hawking set his mind to applying these ideas to the concept of a singularity. His goal was grandiose. He wished to demonstrate that singularities could exist and in fact do exist, and that the origin of the entire universe from such a singularity could be satisfactorily explained.

In this he was inspired by the work of Roger Penrose (b. 1931), the English mathematician, physicist and science philosopher.

Penrose had written a paper postulating that the gravitational pull at the center of a black hole might be so insuperably strong that matter, space and even time itself was compressed into a singularity.

Now for us black holes are the commonplace stuff of science fiction films and novels, but when Hawking was writing his thesis they were little more than mathematical curiosities that had been postulated by the General Theory of Relativity.

Indeed the term 'black hole' was only adopted as a handy descriptive in 1964. At the time there was much theorizing about what the nature of a black hole would be.

Physicists can now tell us how bizarre black holes are, even though they are still shrouded in mystery and there is still much more they don't know about them than what they do know.

A black hole is a collapsed star, though not all stars become black holes. They arise from gigantic stars like red supergiant, which explode as a supernova and then gradually collapse into super-dense masses that exert so powerful a gravitational field that not even light can escape.

Strange things happen in black holes. The ordinary laws of space and time seem to disappear.

Einstein's General Theory of Relativity predicts that gravity curves matter. So if someone were to fall into a black hole they would appear to be stretched out like a piece of elastic.

Now gravity not only curves space, but time too. So something weird would happen to time too.

The closer an object moves toward a black hole the slower it travels in time. When that object reaches the event horizon, the boundary beyond which even light cannot escape, time would slow so much that it would appear to freeze – forever.

However, all this is what an observer would see. They would see, along with everything that was ever drawn by the black hole, a person stretched out and frozen in time.

On another level, the person would no longer exist for they would have been vaporized by the awful power of the black hole.

But suppose that person could survive, and plummeted into the depths of the black hole?

No-one knows. At the center of a black hole space and would be infinitely curved, becoming Penrose's singularity. The laws of the universe as we know them would no longer exist, and no-one knows what that would be like.

In his thesis Hawking proposed that the hypothetical singularity in a yet hypothetical black hole would provide the perfect model for the Big Bang.

Suppose that all the matter that is or ever was in the universe was compressed in a single point. Then that singularity exploded, releasing the matter and formed the universe.

For us the idea of the Big Bang is firmly embedded in the popular imagination, though we should remind ourselves that at the time the Big Bang was controversial, and the existence of black holes was not proven until one was discovered in 1971.

Hawking's thesis was therefore bold and inspiring.

It was so inspiring in fact that after obtaining his doctorate Hawking and Penrose decided to work further on the subject of singularities and the possibility of the universe originating from one.

In 1970 they together published a proof that the universe must have derived from a singularity.

Further theories came thick and fast. With physicists James Bardeen and Brandon Carter he composed a set of laws governing black holes.

Hawking described his research on black holes in his first book, entitled The Large Scale Structure of Space-Time, which he wrote with the mathematician and cosmologist George Ellis in 1973.

In 1974 Hawking accomplished what was perhaps his greatest achievement in the scientific field. In a paper he asserted that the proposition that nothing could escape the gravitational pull of a black hole is not entirely true.

According to Hawking, black holes emit radiation, very slowly and almost imperceptibly. After many eons the loss of energy causes them to shrink. As they shrink they become hotter.

Eventually they become so hot that they explode, and all the matter that has been subsumed into the black holes is released back into the universe.

At first this idea was controversial because it contradicted the widely accepted idea that a black hole was an absolute finality.

The theory of Hawking Radiation, as his idea is called, sees black holes not as the ultimate destroyers in the universe but as engines of creation. Black holes give rise to new stars and galaxies. They are, if you will, the great recyclers of the universe.

Hawking Radiation also answers a question about the universe's probable origin from a single point of singularity, much like a black hole.

If the singularity were a point of infinitely dense matter from which not only light could escape, how could the initial explosion possibly occur? What force could overcome the gravitational pull?

Hawking Radiation neatly avoids that problem by stating a black hole loses positively charged atomic particles at the event horizon, the point around a black hole beyond which the gravitational pull of a black hole is overpowering.

Negatively charged atomic particles continue into the black hole singularity.

The idea has become widely accepted, and it earned Hawking a Fellowship in the famous Royal Society of academics and scientists.

As yet there is unfortunately no direct proof of Hawking Radiation. That is why Hawking has not as yet been offered the Nobel Prize for this idea.

Following his hypothesis about Hawking Radiation Hawking speculated about a terrible possibility. He discussed the possibility that a collapsed black hole might very well wipe out the entire universe.

In a 1993 research paper Hawking supposed that sometimes a black hole that completely evaporates would leave a singularity. A singularity is a point of infinite density.

This singularity might be 'naked', meaning that the event horizon – the point beyond which not even light can escape – has disappeared also.

This means that the awful power of the singularity is exposed. There is nothing to stop the entire universe from being ripped apart by the rapidly spreading singularity

Now black holes take many billions of years to evaporate, and perhaps none ever has. On the other hand, perhaps a naked singularity is presently hurtling toward us.

Even so, it might take many millions of light years to reach us, so we can probably still book that holiday.

Hawking has said he prefers the speculative method in theoretical physics. He prefers to postulate an idea and see if the facts and the math fit his theory.

This means that occasionally he has been wrong, and on some quite important topics. But he has always been prepared to reassess the data at his disposal and admit his mistakes.

Hawking apparently has a penchant for making wagers with his colleagues over scientific questions.

For example, he bet a colleague, Kip Thorne, in 1975 that Cygnus X-1, a source of X-rays in the Cygnus constellation, was not in fact a black hole.

By 1990 it had become widely accepted, based on data that it was a black hole and Hawking conceded the bet.

Thorne's prize was a year's subscription to Penthouse magazine.

In 1975 Hawking was appointed Reader in Gravitational Physics at Cambridge University. By this time his speech was rapidly deteriorating, and he been using a wheelchair for several years.

He refused to concede anything to the disease that ravaged his body, and his family often remarked that he seemed to pretend that it did not exist, sometimes to their frustration.

He was notorious in the wheelchair, recklessly careering down the passages of Cambridge and occasionally running over feet.

After contracting life-threatening pneumonia in 1985 a tracheotomy was performed on him and he lost what remained of his speech.

This necessitated round-the-clock care and the employment of nurses working in three shifts.

It also meant that alternative methods of communication had to be devised.

At first cards were used, but in 1986 his famous voice synthesizer was devised and installed.

The synthesizer has an American accent because it was made in the United States. Hawking regards it as his own voice, and refuses to use any other. In fact, he has patented the voice so no-one else may use it.

At first he chose letters by moving a hand. However he has since lost movement in all but his cheeks and he uses his right cheek to manipulate the device.

From the many, many interviews we see recorded with Stephen Hawking, it appears as though his speech machine works much like a human voice.

Of course, when one considers the matter, this cannot be true.

In fact, speech is very slow, as he controls the machine with facial muscles to operate the sounds.

The impression we see during interviews comes about because Stephen has the questions in advance, and is able to 'pre-record' his answers to them.

Though his body declined his mind remained sharper than ever, and he seemed able to inhabit a world of pure intellect. Often he would spend hours by himself. Afterwards he would say 'I have solved that equation!'

However, he would soon be reminded of the limitations of his own body in a frightening and horrific manner.

Prisoner

In the 80s Stephen and Jane's marriage was breaking down.

Academically they were of different minds. Stephen thrived in the world of mathematical clarity and perfection. Jane enjoyed the comparative freedom and creativity of the humanities. She enjoyed music as well. Neither really understood the pleasures the others found in their disciplines.

Jane had a doctorate in Spanish poetry, and had felt compelled to obtain it in order that she might have an academic life at Cambridge distinct from that of her husband.

Jane was deeply religious. Stephen was, and remains, a firm atheist. At times he mocked her faith.

Jane found his devotion to the 'goddess Physics' ironic, given that it was she who made the decision to keep her husband on life support when he contracted pneumonia.

The doctors had given him up for dead, but Jane had faith that he could survive.

Jane formed a strong but platonic relationship with an organist from the church choir she belonged to. His name was Johnathan Hellyer Jones. Jae would later marry him.

This relationship was apparently accepted by Stephen.

Though devoted to her husband, Jane found attending to the needs of Stephen wearying, especially as he seemed oblivious to his condition and to the demands it made on others.

At length he did agree to hire extra help. University students took on the role of personal assistants and nurses undertook his physical care.

Though this did free Jane to pursue her own interests it also created a new pressure on their relationship.

Accompanied by aides for most of his waking hours Hawking was increasing isolated from his wife's influence.

As carers often do, Hawking's assistants developed a sense of responsibility that resented and excluded the influence of others, even that of his wife and children.

One carer in particular was assuming the position as the primary guardian of Hawking and interpreter of his needs.

This individual was Elaine Mason. She joined Hawking's nursing team in the 1980s. She rapidly assumed the first position in the caring team, excluding all but her own influence.

Hawking and Mason became close, and in 1995 he married her.

After their marriage Hawking's children and friends found themselves unable to approach him without going through Mason, who appeared to control every aspect of Hawking's life.

Then, in 2000, Hawking presented to a local hospital with a broken arm and a split lip. He refused to explain how he had come by them.

In January 2001, just shy of his 60th birthday, he presented again with a broken femur, saying that he had crashed into a wall.

To those who knew him this seemed odd, given that he was so adept in his wheelchair.

Many in Hawking's circle, including some of his nurses, suspected Mason. They spoke of hearing her scream abuse at her husband.

The police were called in by his daughter, Lucy, but Hawking refused to reveal how he sustained a string of injuries, decrying the intrusion into his private life.

On March 29 2004 Cambridge police dropped their investigation of Hawking's injuries, declaring it to be 'extremely thorough.'

However it was noted that only 12 people had been interviewed, and that Hawking himself vehemently denied the allegations that he had been physically abused.

'I firmly and wholeheartedly reject the allegations that I have been assaulted,' he said. In the light of these denials the investigators found themselves stymied.

Friends of Hawking were astonished. One concerned person had reported a conversation with him about Elaine. 'I cannot be left alone with her,' he said. 'Please don't go.'

Why then did Hawking refuse to admit to even his children that he was being assaulted? Given his attitude toward his debility, it may be that he did not want to draw attention to his vulnerability.

Perhaps the hold Elaine Hawking had over him was too strong, and he feared losing her. Relationships of dependency between the abused and their abusers are not uncommon.

On October 20 2006 Stephen and Elaine agreed to divorce. Hawking refused to comment on the divorce, regarding media interest and unwanted distraction, and to this day he has not spoken about the injuries he sustained during their marriage. There is no new investigation.

After their separation Hawking drew closer to his three children and indeed to Jane, who by now was married to Hellyer Jones. Jane always remained interested in and concerned for her ex-husband, and they remain close friends.

A Theory for Everything

Even during his personal trials Hawking remained focused on his academic pursuits. By his 60th birthday he had his mind set on the most ambitious intellectual goal of all – a theory of everything.

The Theory of Everything is the holy grail of theoretical physics. It is conceived as a sort of all-encompassing framework that would explain how everything in the universe works and fits together.

So far scientists have parts of an explanation. The General Theory of Relativity is one part. Quantum mechanics, the study of subatomic particles and their activity, is another. The four laws of thermodynamics governing energy are another.

The ultimate explanation, the glue that binds the myriad of physical laws together, is however missing.

Theoretical physicists aspire to come up with a mathematical equation that will answer everything. It would explain how the universe came into being. In particular it would explain where the initial matter in the came from. It would explain how something came from nothing!

To many, discovering this equation would be the pinnacle achievement of the human race. Scientific knowledge would be complete.

Others are anxious about the quest. They say that attaining such knowledge would be like eating the fruit from the Tree of the Knowledge of Good and Evil in the biblical Garden of Eden. We would become like gods, but terrible and immature in the way we exercise divine power.

For Hawking however there is nothing to fear. The quest for the Theory of Everything is for him the destiny of the human mind, which on Earth is privileged to reflect upon the wonders of creation and ponder their purpose.

He declared that a theory of everything, or Grand Unified Theory, as it is also called, was on the horizon in 1980s. He said that it had a good chance of becoming a reality by the beginning of the 21st century.

The publication of A Brief History of Time in 1988 marked Hawking's first venture into the realms of popular science.

He was approached by Cambridge University Press to write a book for laypeople about the universe and its evolution, using simplified terms and explanations.

Hawking was at first reluctant but he needed the money. He was initially frustrated by the editors, who insisted he keep simplifying his language.

The book popularized the work of Hawking, who until now had been a little known scientist beyond the halls of academia.

Hawking rapidly rose in the estimation of his peers and in 1979 he was appointed Professor to the Lucasian Chair of Mathematics at Cambridge.

This august seat of learning was founded by one Reverend Henry Lucas in 1663, and has been occupied by such intellectual giants as Isaac Newton and the nineteenth century inventor of the computer, Charles Babbage.

Hawking's research style is, by his own admission, more intuitive and speculative than evidence – based.

In other words, he makes informed speculations that seem to fit existing data and looks for the evidence to confirm the idea, rather than draw strict mathematical conclusions from the existing data.

'I would rather be right than rigorous,' he has said. For a scientist this may seem a rather casual way to seek truth. Hawking however sees this as creative. Many of his colleagues have been inspired by his ideas and scour the sky in search of evidence.

He has always been quick to acknowledge when the evidence has proved him wrong.

One instance of Hawking running into controversy with this method concerned a problem called the black hole information paradox.

All matter in the universe has information. By information scientists mean the mathematically quantifiable qualities that matter possesses – size, mass, width, temperature, and so forth.

When matter reaches the event horizon of a black hole it is vaporized, as we have seen. Yet the information of the matter remains.

We will remember when we were discussing black holes. The closer an object, say a spacecraft, approaches the event horizon the slower time becomes. So when it strikes the horizon an observer would still see the spacecraft forever, even though it is actually destroyed.

In other words, the information quantifying that matter would remain.

It's a tough concept to get the mind around. Even scientists have difficulty explaining it. But it makes sense mathematically given Einstein's theories of relativity.

However Hawking proposed in his theory of Hawking Radiation that a black hole very gradually evaporates, and that eventually it will disappear entirely.

But if that happened, where does the information of the spacecraft go? Does it disappear as well?

This was a problem for physicists, because it is a well-founded dogma of physics that information cannot be destroyed.

Hawking acknowledge the paradox and came up with a solution. He suggested that the information contained in matter falling into a black hole was preserved and released back into the universe by the outgoing Hawking Radiation.

However, this is a hunch on Hawking's part. It is unproven, just as Hawking Radiation itself remains unproven. Mathematically it is satisfying idea for many physicists. Yet there remains no concrete evidence to confirm the idea.

Hawking also courted controversy with the physicist Peter Higgs, over the latter's postulation of a universal field which gives everything in the universe mass.

Hawking strongly disputed the existence of such a field, until a particle of the field, the Higgs boson, was discovered by the powerful Hadron collider in Switzerland in 2013.

The so-called 'God particle' gives being to everything I the universe. Peter Higgs was awarded the Nobel Prize for predicting the existence of the Higgs boson and Higgs field in 2013.

Stephen Hawking was absolutely convinced that such a particle could not exist, and even bet with a colleague, Gordon Kane, that it would never be discovered.

Even after it was discovered he lamented its existence, complaining that it made physics less interesting.

He even suggested that the Higgs particle could mean the literal doom of the universe. While admitting the existence of the Higgs Field he suggested that it might at some point become unstable ad vaporize the universe.

While this may sound like sour grapes on Hawking's part, he has actually never been so petty as to deny evidence-based discoveries by his colleagues, even if Peter Higgs was awarded the Nobel Prize.

The discovery of the Higgs Field does however highlight Hawking's academic style and explain why he has never received the Nobel Prize himself, and perhaps never will attain that honor.

Hawking's research is highly creative. He prefers to speculate. Nobel Prizes are only given for proven scientific discoveries. Hawking Radiation, Hawking's greatest hypothesis, though widely accepted by scientists, remains an albeit highly informed mathematical speculation. No evidence has ever been discovered to confirm or deny its existence.

Hawking's creative mind impels him to make contributions beyond his field of theoretical physics. This is ironic, given that the scientists who could not be his postgraduate mentor, Fred Hoyle, proved unsuitable precisely because he too ventured into other realms.

Like Hawking, Hoyle was often before a camera presenting science to the public.

Hawking has warned humanity about creating an artificial intelligence that could be self-aware. Such an entity, he says, would assume an existence separated from humanity, evolve by itself and possibly enslave or destroy humanity in a horrendous Matrix or Terminator scenario.

He speaks about climate change and overpopulation and the diminution of Earth's resources.

He believes that Earth' resources could be consumed within around 100 years and then the human species will face extinction.

His solution is to colonize another world, and so he encourages the exploration of other solar systems and the development of technologies to transport humans to habitable planets in them.

The idea is not so outlandish as it may seem at first. Recent astronomical observations have indicated the existence of planets orbiting nearby stars. Some of these planets are similar to Earth in that they are not too close to their sun and not too far away as to make life impossible.

Hawking is a keen supporter of the Breakthrough Initiatives, a series of programs founded ad funded by the Russian entrepreneur Yuri Milner I 2015 to seek out habitable worlds and develop the technology to colonize them.

The Initiatives also hope to discover extraterrestrial life, and Hawking seems less keen on this venture.

Hawking's attitude to the possible of life on other worlds is cool and logical. He remains a skeptic about the existence of a deity. He believes the universe does not need one, and that eventually the human mind will be able to explain everything.

So for Hawking life is the result of a series of chance happenings, though no less wonderful for that.

Life on Earth then is statistically highly improbable. Life on other worlds must then be even more improbable still, and it remains possible that we are alone in the universe.

But if there are other intelligent life forms in the universe Hawking is not too keen to meet them.

If they are like us, he argues, and more technologically advanced than us, they have likely used up the resources on their own planet and have started to use the resources of others.

If they were to discover our world, they would most likely wish to colonize it, in much the same way that Europeans colonized the New World.

For Hawking intelligent life, whether it be biological or an artificial intelligence, is parasitical, controlling resources and fighting for control of them.

He does not approve of such behavior. He simple acknowledges it as an inevitably.

This nevertheless presents a rather pessimistic view of the concept of civilization, though it would seem to be borne out by facts.

Pessimistic though his views about humanity are it is probably fair to comment that he is encouraging people to talk about the problems that face our planet.

Back in the world of theoretical physics, Hawking's views were shifting. In 2010 he and Leonard Mlodinow published The Grand Design, a book covering the evolution of modern physics and cosmology.

In this book Hawking abandons his idea of finding a single explanation of the universe.

Instead he claims that there are five explanations.

His ideas are based on the supposition of minute, unobservable subatomic particles called strings. These strings vibrate in different modulations and each modulation represents a different state of being. And so the same string could have a number of alternate and simultaneous realities.

Each string theory has 11 dimensions, meaning that there are multiple alternate realities in the universe, each as true as the other, and consequently multiple explanations of reality.

This extraordinary and almost incomprehensible idea has been called M-Theory. The name is enigmatic, and the M has been interpreted as standing for 'magic' or 'mystery.'

However, like all Hawking's great ideas, it remains an informed hunch. It excites physicists, many of whom are striving to confirm it and solve some of the problems it presents.

From these ideas Hawking extrapolated one about the origin of the universe. It is useless, he postulated, to attempt to determine the origin of the universe, because it had a multitude of different origins.

This is based on the strange science of quantum mechanics, the workings of particles smaller than atoms. There the laws of physics as we know them in the macro world do not apply. There is a whole new set of laws that physicists are still only beginning to discover.

In the mysterious world of quantum particles different realities can co-exist. Indeed, this new field of research is exploding old ideas about the nature of space and time.

It has been suggested that time itself is not linear, flowing from the past through the present and into the future like a stream. Rather it may be the past and future occurs side by side in alternate but co-existing realities.

Time travel is another popular subject on which Hawking has been happy to speak.

He says that travel into the future is certainly possible. Indeed, it happens all the time.

The General Theory of Relativity holds that the closer an object approaches the speed of light the more it moves into the future relative to its starting point. In other words, time for that object s slows down.

So if a rocket or spaceship could be powered by a drive that would approximate the speed of light (according to the principles of relativity an object cannot supersede the speed of light) it could theoretically project an occupant forward in time.

Yet there would be a problem, in that the faster the craft went, the more mass it would take on .If a craft were theoretically able to fly at just short of the speed of light it would be so massive that the universe could scarcely contain it.

What of travelling in the past? According to the Einstein's General Law of Relativity, time can only travel forwards, not backwards.

However, there may theoretically be a way to travel through time. Hawking and other theoretical physicists speculate that a black hole could create a wormhole.

A wormhole would be a link between two points in space-time. But scientists have no idea how you would use such a portal. Firstly you would have to somehow avoid being crushed by the colossal power of a black hole.

Secondly, there is no way to predict what would happen, nor how a wormhole could be engineered to transport a person or object to a given point in space and time.

And even supposing it was possible to harness the power of a black hole to travel back in time would we want to?

Travelling backwards in time could create paradoxes. Suppose a person goes back in time and inadvertently kills his or own father before he was born?

If he kills his father he cannot exist. How then could he have gone back in time and killed him?

Hawking does not like that possibility. It disturbs the idea of an ordered, logical universe, and he has invented a law to stop it happening.

Tongue in cheek, he has proposed that quantum particles would instantly incinerate a time machine to prevent such a paradox being created.

But in typical fashion he presents a simple fact to dismiss the idea of travel into the past. If it is possible to travel backwards in time, where are the time travelers? Where are the tourists who have come to visit the past?

Perhaps they have come, and we have had them sectioned. Or perhaps they are in disguise, under strict instructions not to interfere in history.

Hawking conducted an experiment to determine once and for all whether time travel into the past was possible.

He held a party for time travelers. He posted the open invitation on YouTube. It read 'You are cordially invited to a reception for time travelers hosted by Stephen Hawking to be held at the University of Cambridge.'

He included geographical co-ordinates and the date, adding 'no RSVP required.'

However, he did not post the invitation until after the date.

He prepared a room with balloons, champagne and nibbles and waited.

Alas, no-one turned up.

World's Greatest Living Genius?

In the popular imagination Stephen Hawking is perhaps the greatest living mind. Indeed one would be hard-pressed to think of any other scientist who has captured the attention of the world as much as Stephen Hawking.

There is the physicist Brian Cox, well-known as a presenter and writer of popular science. However his own contribution to physics is relatively small.

Likewise if we move beyond physics and consider biology, we can consider Richard

Dawkins, known primarily not for science at all but for his criticism of religion.

In contrast Hawking stands out not only for his popular explanations of science via television and the printed word but for the substance of his ideas.

His grandest idea concerns the fundamental and universal question every human being has asked – how did the universe come into being?

Hawking explained to the world, through his work on black holes, how the entire cosmos was flung out of a singularity.

We might ask ourselves however, as critics have, how the science expounded by

Hawking has been conflated with celebrity appeal. Is it possible to critique his ideas without critiquing the personality behind those ideas?

Critics remind us that his greatest ideas, inspiring though they may be and framed by brilliant calculations, are largely intuitive hypotheses, yet unproven.

Hawking Radiation remains unproven, and scientists have pointed out huge problems even in his idea of the Big Bang.

First there is the problem of where the matter dormant in the singularity came from. Hawking hopes to demonstrate sometime in the future how something can come from nothing, but for now it remains a difficulty.

Some researchers point out that the Big Bang seems to violate the Law of Entropy, which says that matter becomes less organized over time. Yet if this is so how do the stars and galaxies seem to be so incredibly complex and organized?

There are, after all, scientific alternatives to the Big Bang theory. Some scientists postulate a Big Bounce rather than a Big Bang. In this model our universe is one of an infinite series of contracting and expanding universes, neatly avoiding the problem of creation from nothing.

There are other theories as well. And yet the Big Bang remains the first, and for many the only, known theory of the universe. Few persons apart from physicists seem able to fully grasp the concept, and yet it has gripped the world.

Are we listening to the man rather than the idea? Has Hawking become some sort of demagogue, the high priest of science?

We are reminded too that Hawking has been wrong on a number of occasions and has freely admitted this.

And then we should consider the elephant in the room. Stephen Hawking is a man who lives in his own mind. His brain is the prisoner of a body that no longer obeys it. Or to put it another way, his mind has been freed from the distractions of the body and the demands of the flesh.

So has Hawking become for us a sort of scientific saint? Is he a mental ascetic, transported by the denial of the flesh to some higher plane we mere mortals can only dream of?

Doubtless Hawking himself would balk at the suggestion, but perhaps we are projecting our own conceptions of genius and disability upon him, and unfairly so.

Hawking has never wanted to be seen as disabled, but perhaps the perception of genius in him enables us to frame him within our own flawed, romanticized ideas of what disability means.

Perhaps unconsciously we are influenced by the romantic idea of the savant, the individual limited in one aspect, yet gifted by nature in another by way of compensation.

Hawking would certainly not thank us for this back-handed compliment, nor agree with the logic of that idea. He does not believe there is justice inherent in the universe. There is only the inevitable flow of course and effect, without intent or purpose.

Hawking rarely talks about himself, and almost never speaks about his feelings. However he did speak on the relationship between his illness and his work.

'When you are faced with the possibility of early death,' he said, 'it makes you realize life's worth living, and there are lots of things you want to do.'

He is not trying to beat death, but rather to live each day as fully as he can, which is great advice for anyone.

He says he does not play to the media, nor use it to spruce his ideas. The purpose of his media appearances and books (he even wrote a series for children with his daughter Lucy) is simply to explain his work to the public, something he considers important.

He admits that his research won't affect the daily lives of people very much at all. Black holes, string theory and quantum mechanics won't cure diseases or end famine or bring world peace, 'but it is important to understand where we come from and what we can expect to find as we explore.'

It does not appear that Hawking is a theoretical physicist for the fame and glory. He does what he does because he loves it.

So could it be that he does not want to share his genius with the world? He doesn't want to prove anything. He's just a guy using his talents and having a great time doing it.

The Theory of Everything and Other Media Portrayals

In 2014, two films were released in the United Kingdom which, at first glance, appeared unlikely to make any kind of impact on the cinema going public.

The reason for this was their subject matter – in both cases, they focused on the lives of true British Heroes.

But very much not of the James Bond kind. No, the subject of these films was intellectual geniuses who had made their mark on the culture and history of the country.

That the lead actors in these films were two of the bright young sparks of English acting added to the appeal.

And that they had attended well known, competing public schools further raised the anticipation.

The comparisons between Eddie Redmayne playing Stephen Hawking in 'The Theory of Everything' and Benedict Cumberbatch's portrayal of Alan Turing in 'The Imitation Game' became the talked about thing in British cinema.

Redmayne is an old Etonian. Whilst there, he had once played the back end of an Elephant in a house play.

By contrast, Cumberbatch is an old Harrovian. The two schools are competitors. Geographically they are quite close – Harrow being in North London, Eton just to the West of Heathrow.

They compete over their alumni. Eton might throw former Prime Minister David Cameron but Harrow can trump with Winston Churchill (although, apparently, he hated the school).

Eton counters with the Royal Princes, Harrow check mates with…Winston Churchill.

Turing, the subject of Benedict Cumberbatch's film, was the mathematical genius who solved the enigma code.

This was the machine Germans used during the Second World War to send out messages to its navy operators, and from which they would launch attacks on convoys crossing the Atlantic.

Turing worked at Bletchley Park, a converted manor house in the center of England from where code breakers operated during the war.

He created the machine which was able to interpret the German Enigma codes, solve them and, many would argue, lead the allies to victory in the war.

'The Imitation Game' is a great film, but it was trumped by the unlikely success of a film about a disabled scientist.

Eddie Redmayne described the challenges of playing Stephen Hawking, for which he won an Oscar.

Firstly, his burgeoning admiration for the man presented its own problems. He had spent six months researching into Hawking, and became gradually to see the scientist as an idol.

So when they met for the first time, he spewed a nervous barrage of conversation at his subject, his anxiety and delight at meeting his new hero combining to make him virtually unintelligible.

During the research phase, Redmayne was extremely thorough.

He visited victims of amyotrophic lateral sclerosis (motor-neurone disease). In fact, he spent four months at the National Hospital for Neurology and Neurosurgery's clinic learning about the condition.

He talked to Stephen's family. He read (without full comprehension) 'A Brief History of Time'. He watched footage of his subject.

The film was to be about Hawking's university days, when he both met his wife and inspiration, Jane Wilde, and when he contracted the life destroying medical condition.

He had wanted to be as prepared as possible before meeting the great man, but now

Redmayne was about to be introduced to the person he would be playing, he began to have doubts.

What if the research he had undertaken had given him a false impression of the scientist?

But, once he had calmed himself, Redmayne learned much from the meeting.

He discovered that Stephen's voice had become extremely slurry during the onset of his disease.

The presented a problem that he and the director, James Marsh, had not really considered. They were left with a conundrum.

On the one hand, they wished to represent Hawking and his condition in as honest a light as possible, but equally they did have to produce something their audience could understand.

It is all very well being true to the story, but if the audience cannot understand it, then that story is not being told.

Subtitles were a possibility discussed. But both director and actor felt that these would detract from, rather than clarify, the tale they wished to tell.

The resulting speech added much to the power of the story.

Another thing that Eddie Redmayne had not fully grasped was the humor and vitality of the scientist.

Although physically he is able to use only a very small number of muscles, the cheeky, energetic and offbeat humor of the eleven year old starting out at St Albans School back in the 1950s is still present.

It was the addition of this that enabled the story to be a powerful tug on the emotions, rather than a maudlin tale.

Redmayne worked with a dance teacher to train his body to be able to adopt the uncomfortable positions into which Stephen's body has contorted.

It was important to do this first. After all, Redmayne would also be portraying a character in love, and it was important that the physical factors did not detract from his concentration on this.

He learned that one thing suffers from the condition do is to concentrate as much into their few remaining active muscles as possible.

These become conduits for expressing their emotions, and showing themselves.

With Stephen Hawking, it was his face, and especially his eyebrows, that continued to show the real man.

Redmayne worked hard, studying footage extensively, to try to capture how these normally insignificant facial features worked.

However, 'The Theory of Everything' is not the only occasion in which Stephen Hawking has appeared on film.

Not by a long chalk.

It is a part of his appeal that he is so media friendly. After all, most of us would probably struggle to name any other living scientists, but Stephen's name would be first on the lips during any quiz.

Perhaps one of his most famous roles has been in TV's hit cartoon comedy, 'The Simpsons'.

Stephen's daughter, Lucy, knows one of the scriptwriters on the US show, and learned that they wanted to write an episode featuring the scientist.

She persuaded her father to take part. He voiced himself to his cartoon presence a number of times.

He appeared in the season 10 episode, 'They Saved Lisa's Brain', which was also used in archive footage in a season 11 episode.

He also took part in several more performances. These include the season 16 episode 'Don't Fear the Roofer'; season 18's 'Stop or My Dog Will Shoot!' and the season 22 show 'Elementary School Musical'.

Stephen also appeared in a documentary special – 'The Simpsons: A Culture Show'.

Given the longevity of the show, and the desire of world renowned figures from popular culture to be involved, it is another remarkable achievement that Stephen appears in the top 20 of IGN's 'Top 25 Simpsons Guest Stars'.

He rolls in at number 16 – quite remarkable for a cosmologist.

Stephen wrote the 2010 mini-series 'Into the Universe with Stephen Hawking'. This series was created for the discovery channel. It aired both in the US and in Britain.

However, in Britain, it was known as 'Stephen Hawking's Universe.'

With a neat touch of irony, voice overs were recorded by the actor Benedict Cumberbatch, who would of course be the lead in the rival film to Eddie Redmayne's 'The Theory of Everything' in a few years' time.

In the science series, Hawking appears in person in each of the episodes – 'Aliens', 'Time Trael' and 'The Story of Everything'.

In the last of these, some footage was used for an episode of another documentary, 'Curiosity'.

'Star Trek' is, as we all know, one of the great science fiction series of all time, and in this Stephen Hawking created a 'first'.

In the episode 'Descent, Part 1' – the denouement of Season Six of 'Star Trek: The Next Generation' he appears as a hologram.

He is shown playing poker with two other fairly recognizable names from the world of science, Sir Isaac Newton and Albert Einstein.

However, the notable point about this is that he played the hologram himself. In doing so he became the first ever guest on 'Star Trek' to play himself.

Just as with 'The Simpsons', and the ironic portrayal of card playing on 'Star Trek', comedy is one of Stephen's favorite genres for film and TV.

Not surprising, perhaps, given his generally funny demeanour.

He appeared in the British TV comedy legend 'Red Dwarf'. Stephen is a fan of the series, and has praised the writers for their witty use of faux-science.

He has also taken part in the huge US science based comedy show 'The Big Bang Theory', which stars Jim Parsons.

He has appeared in no fewer than six episodes, often as a voice over. The episodes are:

'The Hawking Excitation', The Extract Obliteration', 'The Relationship Diremption', 'The Troll Manifestation', 'The Celebration Experimentation' and 'The Geology Elevation'.

Most years in the United Kingdom, a large charity event is held called Red Nose Day.

Created by comedian Lenny Henry as a way to tackle poverty in Africa, the charity is now a part of British Culture.

It features various zany events taking place around the country, and stars appear on the live show, where people pledge money.

Often in return for those stars doing something funny, but undignified. Each year, a new design of Red Nose is created, plus versions for your car.

With enormous self-irony, Hawking appeared in 2015 in which he 'transforms' into a 'Transformer'.

The sketch featured two cutting edge British comedians alongside Hawking – Catherine Tate and David Walliams.

He also took part in a sketch with Jim Carrey on 'Late Night with Conan O'Brien'. The left field, slightly seditious 'TV Offal' featured him in the title sequence.

Other appearances on TV include presenting the trophy for the winners of the tough quiz show, University Challenge.

He has been involved in numerous science based documentaries including 'Genius of Britain', where he was link man for a series on famous British Scientists.

He was a participant in the documentary 'The 11th Hour' and 'Alien Planet'. He also hosted, through voice over, a science fiction series 'Masters of Science Fiction.'

Hawking's first connection with the actor Benedict Cumberbatch happened during the filming of the TV Movie 'Hawking'.

With surprising similarity to the major Hollywood film some years later, this film too portrayed Stephen's time Cambridge.

Cumberbatch played the eponymous lead in the film.

Stephen was also portrayed by an actor in an episode of 'Stargate Atlantis'. 'Brain Storm' and as well in 'Superhero Movie.'

On top of his various appearances in 'The Simpsons', he is also a regular in 'Futurama', having been a character in the following episodes.

In 'Anthology of Interest' he appears as a guard of the space-time continuum. 'The Beast with a Billion Backs' he has a somewhat curtailed role as he is shown as simply a head in a jar.

'Family Guy' is another cartoon show which has drawn heavily on Hawking. He has appeared in seven episodes, most recently as a streaker in a basketball game.

He is a video game character in the episode entitled 'reincarnation'.

Such is his recognizable voice, and so well and warmly is he regarded, that he is often subject to gentle parody, particularly in British comedy shows.

A character from the hit series 'The Vicar of Dibley', Frank (whose character is renowned for being boring) chooses to portray his role as a Wise Man in a Nativity play as having Hawking's voice.

Keeping with the faux-religious theme, he is referenced in the comedy 'Father Ted.'

Other times he has been referred to in a similar way include the American hit 'Seinfeld' amongst many others.

He has appeared widely in commercials; include some for the high end marque Jaguar.

Stephen also pre-recorded an amusing skit featuring his wheel chair for a Monty Python show.

In fact, his media appearances and representations are myriad. Amongst the enormous number not listed here is the use of his voice on a Pink Floyd album.

Perhaps one of his favorite lampoonings involved the satirical news publication 'The Onion'.

In it the periodical runs an article claiming that Hawking has designed a high powered robotic exoskeleton.

In keeping with his love of a joke, Stephen wrote a letter published in the paper in which he claims that they have unveiled his plans for world domination.

It is remarkable, and of enormous merit, that a man so physically afflicted could encounter life with such positivity and sense of fun.

Hawking is also a prolific writer. Some of his works have been discussed already in this book, but in fact he has produced no fewer than twenty-six publications for which he is either co or sole writer.

This is in addition to the far too many to mention articles he has written.

As a closing point for this biography, we will look at a collection of eight of these books which might well slip under the net.

Co-written with his daughter Lucy, Stephen has produced this mini collection written specifically for children.

The 'George' series feature George and his best friend Annie. The intrepid duo travel into space, learning (as is the case with their readers as well) about scientific principles as they go.

The stories capture the off-beat, funny and creative side of Stephen which we saw right back from a young child, when he would abandon Monopoly for games of his own, complex, making.

An example of the creativity in the George books can be taken from their 2014 publication 'George and the Unbreakable Code'.

In this wonderful story, we see the libertarian, anti-establishment Hawking shine through. Banks hand out free money, supermarkets stop being able to charge for food and aircraft refuse to fly.

All because super computers appear to have been hacked.

In another of their books, 'George and the Big Bang', he demonstrates the respect for young people that will always win their adoration.

He explores one of his most complex theories despite the youth of his audience.

Here, George is having a few domestic problems and even his best friend Anne seems to have other things on her mind.

So, he sets out to help another mate, Eric, develop his plans to go back to the beginning of the universe.

The story features evil doing villains and takes the form of a story, collection of essays and even a graphic novel element.

'George's Secret Key to the Universe' explores physics, science and the universe as a whole through a thrilling series of adventures.

In this story, a super computer with its own intelligence (called Cosmos) takes Annie, her father Eric and, of course, George on an exciting trip to the edge of a black hole – and hopefully home again.

The theory of black holes explained through comedy and adventure.

Brilliant.

Stephen Hawking is not just a genius. He is an educator and a man with a razor sharp wit and enormous sense of fun.

In his own words

My advice to other disabled people would be, concentrate on things your disability doesn't prevent you doing well, and don't regret the things it interferes with. Don't be disabled in spirit as well as physically.

No one undertakes research in physics with the intention of winning a prize. It is the joy of discovering something no one knew before.

Science is beautiful when it makes simple explanations of phenomena or connections between different observations. Examples include the double helix in biology and the fundamental equations of physics.

While physics and mathematics may tell us how the universe began, they are not much use in predicting human behavior because there are far too many equations to solve. I'm no better than anyone else at understanding what makes people tick, particularly women.

I regard the brain as a computer which will stop working when its components fail. There is no heaven or afterlife for broken down computers; that is a fairy story for people afraid of the dark.

I was never top of the class at school, but my classmates must have seen potential in me, because my nickname was 'Einstein.'

It is generally recognized that women are better than men at languages, personal relations and multi-tasking, but less good at map-reading and spatial awareness. It is therefore not unreasonable to suppose that women might be less good at mathematics and physics.

A few years ago, the city council of Monza, Italy, barred pet owners from keeping goldfish in curved bowls... saying that it is cruel to keep a fish in a bowl with curved sides because, gazing out, the fish would have a distorted view of reality. But how do we know we have the true, undistorted picture of reality?

Obviously, because of my disability, I need assistance. But I have always tried to overcome the limitations of my condition and lead as full a life as possible. I have travelled the world, from the Antarctic to zero gravity.

God may exist, but science can explain the universe without the need for a creator.

In less than a hundred years, we have found a new way to think of ourselves. From sitting at the center of the universe, we now find ourselves orbiting an average-sized sun, which is just one of millions of stars in our own Milky Way galaxy. Stephen Hawking

The human race may be the only intelligent beings in the galaxy.

I think computer viruses should count as life. I think it says something about human nature that the only form of life we have created so far is purely destructive. We've created life in our own image.

If the rate of expansion one second after the Big Bang had been smaller by even one part in a hundred thousand million, it would have re-collapsed before it reached its present size. On the other hand, if it had been greater by a part in a million, the universe would have expanded too rapidly for stars and planets to form.

I don't have much positive to say about motor neuron disease, but it taught me not to pity myself because others were worse off, and to get on with what I still could do. I'm happier now than before I developed the condition.

We are just an advanced breed of monkeys on a minor planet of a very average star. But we can understand the Universe. That makes us something very special.

The usual approach of science of constructing a mathematical model cannot answer the questions of why there should be a universe for the model to describe. Why does the universe go to all the bother of existing?

God not only plays dice, He also sometimes throws the dice where they cannot be seen.

I believe everyone should have a broad picture of how the universe operates and our place in it. It is a basic human desire. And it also puts our worries in perspective. Stephen Hawking

Science is increasingly answering questions that used to be the province of religion.

It's time to commit to finding the answer, to search for life beyond Earth. Mankind has a deep need to explore, to learn, to know. We also happen to be sociable creatures. It is important for us to know if we are alone in the dark.

My discovery that black holes emit radiation raised serious problems of consistency with the rest of physics. I have now resolved these problems, but the answer turned out to be not what I expected.

I can't disguise myself with a wig and dark glasses - the wheelchair gives me away.

If we do discover a complete theory, it should be in time understandable in broad principle by everyone. Then we shall all, philosophers, scientists, and just ordinary people be able to take part in the discussion of why we and the universe exist.

I think the brain is essentially a computer and consciousness is like a computer program. It will cease to run when the computer is turned off. Theoretically, it could be re-created on a neural network, but that would be very difficult, as it would require all one's memories.

I'm not afraid of death, but I'm in no hurry to die. I have so much I want to do first.

The radiation left over from the Big Bang is the same as that in your microwave oven but very much less powerful. It would heat your pizza only to minus 271.3*C - not much good for defrosting the pizza, let alone cooking it.
Stephen Hawking

I was not a good student. I did not spend much time at college; I was too busy enjoying myself.

So long as the universe had a beginning, we could suppose it had a creator. But if the universe is really completely self-contained, having no boundary or edge, it would have neither beginning nor end: it would simply be. What place, then, for a creator?

Before I lost my voice, it was slurred, so only those close to me could understand, but with the computer voice, I found I could give popular lectures. I enjoy communicating science. It is important that the public understands basic science, if they are not to leave vital decisions to others.

We must develop as quickly as possible technologies that make possible a direct connection between brain and computer, so that artificial brains contribute to human intelligence rather than opposing it.

Even if there is only one possible unified theory, it is just a set of rules and equations. What is it that breathes fire into the equations and makes a universe for them to describe?

Made in the USA
Middletown, DE
08 July 2018